CU00329024

a Book of Short Prayers

Graham Smith

VERITAS

GRAHAM SMITH

A Book of

Short Prayers

VERITAS

First published 1977 by
Veritas Publications
7-8 Lower Abbey Street
Dublin 1

This edition published 1996

ISBN 1 85390 365 5

Acknowledgement
The following prayers appeared in Fairacres
Publication 89 *Short Prayers* (1984, reprinted 1993)
and are reproduced here by kind permission of the
Sisters of the Love of God, Fairacres, Oxford:
24-28; 73; 85; 99; 130; 159-164; 181-185; 271-273;
278-279; 306-308; 312; 317.

Cover Design by Banahan McManus
Printed in the Republic of Ireland by
Paceprint Ltd, Dublin

CONTENTS

INTRODUCTION

I was introduced to collections of short prayers by a little book with the charming title *The Ideot's Devotion* by Dame Gertrude More, a seventeenth century Benedictine nun and great great granddaughter of St Thomas More. I then discovered a 'pool' of such prayers in the Benedictine community, notably in Blosius (sixteenth century) and Augustine Baker, Gertrude More's spiritual director; together with an earlier Benedictine, St Gertrude (1263-1334), whose 'Exercises' breathe the same spirit, and are quoted many times in the present collection.

However, the 'short prayer tradition' goes back through the early Church to the book of Psalms, and petitions in the Gospels, such as the cry 'Lord, help me!' And the greatest prayer of all, the Our Father, can be regarded as a series of such prayers. I began to make my own collection of short prayers in 1959 and this book is a selection of these. Most arose as a result of a prayer exercise. Some are (more or less exact) quotations, which I have sometimes modified or modernised. These are marked with an asterisk, and the sources given in the Appendix. The book is divided into eight parts and the themes follow a logical sequence. Some of the prayers are in close sequence, especially those relating to the Passion and Resurrection of Christ.

Short prayers can help 'that intentness, watchfully alert, which is above all needful to him who prays' (St Augustine). They may help a person 'get into' meditative prayer and the simplification of prayer which is conducive to contemplation. There is impressive testimony from authorities on the spiritual life, e.g. 'We ... should make short but frequent prayers' (Abbot Isaac, fourth century); 'Our prayer should be pure and short' (Rule of St Benedict, sixth century); the fourteenth-century classic *Cloud of Unknowing* recommends the use of few words, 'the fewer the better'; the Russian Orthodox classic *Way of a Pilgrim* advises that we 'choose some short prayer, consisting of few but forcible words, and repeat it frequently and for a long while'. The Lord himself in the Gospel warns us not to 'babble as the pagans do, for they think that by using many words they will make themselves heard' (Matthew 6:7).

The prayers in this collection are meant for individual use, although I hope they are informed by a corporate sense of belonging to a community, and many, perhaps most, of those which are in the singular can easily be put into the plural. Individual prayer always carries with it the danger of pietism and self-cultivation which can become self-indulgent or even downright selfish. To this objection I think the reply is as follows.

The teaching and example of the Lord himself is clear and unequivocal. The prayer of the individual is necessary. We are told in the same passage in the Sermon on the Mount already quoted, 'when you pray, go into your room and shut the door and pray to your Father who is in secret' (Matthew 6:6). Nothing could be more unmistakably 'devotional' than that. Jesus himself at times withdrew from the crowds and even from his disciples, to be alone in a 'lonely place' (Mark 1:35) in order to pray.

At the same time, the custom and practice of the Lord and his followers, and the supreme example of the teaching of the Our Father, with its plural form and corporate spirit, places prayer within the context of fellowship. Both dimensions are necessary, the 'common' prayer and the individual prayer. Living a human life, and certainly living a Christian life, is a team game. We take our part in the game together and in the training and work-outs which accompany it; but we need to do individual training as well; without that, we cannot play our full part in the team game.

How should this book be used? I see it as a vade-mecum, a companion, a handy book to be slipped into the pocket or handbag or cassock, to be used in times of prayer and devotion, and at those odd moments in the day, at work or at home or around and about (waiting for a bus, for example) when opportunity offers. Use it like a little working manual, mark prayers or pages which you like. Select as you will. You might start making your own collection – no literary gift is required!

An old friend of mine, many years ago, was involved in a serious car accident. In a letter afterwards he wrote 'when I was crawling in search of help ... I know that such prayers are those which really give you comfort and hope'. I am sure he did not get a book of prayers out of his pocket as he crawled along, and he may not have remembered any particular prayer. But it is significant that he associated such prayers with a critical situation, and found them meaningful.

Graham Smith

GOD

1   Before the beginning
after the ending
you
God.

2   My God, my God, my all,
you are beyond all
you are all.

3   God,
depth of my life
depth of life.

4*   Father,
you have delivered us
from the dominion of darkness
and transferred us
to the kingdom
of your beloved Son.

5   Father,
you have sent
the Spirit of your Son
into our hearts
crying 'Abba, Father!'

6   Father,
      you gave us,
      you give us
      your Son, your only Son, your Beloved
      May your Kingdom come.

7   Father,
      by the Holy Spirit
      reveal your Son
      in us.

8   Father,
      this is your beloved Son
      in whom you are well pleased.

9*   Father,
      I ask you
      from the wealth of your glory
      strengthen us with power
      by your Spirit
      in our hearts.

      That Christ may dwell
      in our hearts
      by faith.

That we may be
rooted and based in love.

That together with all saints
we may be able to understand
the breadth and length
height and depth

to know what is beyond knowledge –
the love of Christ
and so be completely filled
with the fullness of God.

10   Father,
in the name of Jesus
I ask for the Holy Spirit.

11   Father,
in the name of Jesus
I pray for your Holy Spirit
over all.

12   Love,
in the name of incarnate love
I ask for the energy of love.

13*   Father,
glorify your name.

14* Father,
     glorify your Son
     that the Son may glorify you.

15   Father,
     glorify your name
     glorify your Son
     even in us
     so that even through us
     the Son may glorify you.

16   Here is the secret source
     of this day ... my life ... my
     death ... my life.

17   Jesus,
     baptise us
     with the Spirit
     and with fire.

18* Lord God,
     you are not only my creator
     but also my redeemer.
     Renew your Holy Spirit
     within me this day.

19* Father,
in the name of Jesus
I ask for the wisdom of the Holy Spirit
which is pure and peaceable,
considerate and open to reason,
full of mercy and good fruits,
straightforward and sincere.

20* Blessed be the God and Father
of our Lord Jesus Christ,
the Father of mercies
and God of all comfort.

21* I rejoice in the Holy Spirit
and in union with Jesus in me.
I thank you, Father,
Lord of heaven and earth.

22* Lord,
Father and God of my life.

23 Prayer of Jesus
rise up in my heart
to the Father,
prayer of the Spirit.

24 Make my divided self
whole and one,
Blessed Three in One.

25 God,
   let me be pierced, penetrated,
   permeated by you.

26 Prayer of Jesus in me,
   prayer of the Spirit,
   you are the prayer of God to God.

27 Blest Spirit, you are praying for us.
   Jesus Christ, the Son of God,
   you are praying for us.

   If the Spirit prays
   and the Son prays
   then what does that make prayer?

28 To the Glory
   beyond the Glory
   to the Wholly Other.

29 God from God
   God in man
   man in God
   God in God
   God beyond God.

30 From within
   within me
   within the world
   you work outwards
   my God.

31 Because you are wholly other
   you are wholly present.

32 Jesus in the heart of Mary
   Jesus in my heart
   God in the heart of creatures
   of all creation.

33* Infinite life
   eternal light.

34 Manifest yourself
   in other(s)
   in me
   in yourself.

35 You are greater than it.
   What?
   Anything.

36 You are in this
    but
    greater than this
    you are in that
    but
    greater than that
    you are in all
    but
    greater than all.

37 You are in this
    this is in you
    and you are greater than it.

    You are in that
    that is in you
    and you are greater than it.

    You are in life
    life is in you
    and you are greater than it.

    You are in everything
    everything is in you
    and you are greater than it.

15

Greater than it
greater than all
in the name of Jesus I say
you are greater than it.

38   You are the
addressability of things
connectedness of things
relatedness of things
oneness of things
you are the irreducible.

39   How you are
is how it is.

40   You are the
thisness of things
the thatness of things
the thou-art-ness of things.

41   In consciously receiving this
I receive by faith
somehow
you.

42　Just this
　　in this
　　through this
　　you,
　　my God.

43　You, Jesus,
　　were on the cross
　　you, Triune God,
　　were in the cross.

CHRIST

44* You who are holy
   admirable among all holy ones.
   You whom the whole universe
   pursues with one sole desire.

   You in whom was brought to being
   this miracle
   of all power in a man
   and humility in a God.

   There is not and there never will be
   one like you.
   God,
   my own.

45 Jesus,
   you are
   the tent of the meeting.

46* I it am *(Jesus to Julian of Norwich)*
   You are it

47 Wonder of wonders,
   Jesus,
   your relationship
   with the Father.

48   Jesus,
      Child of God,
      Son of the Father,
      Servant of the Lord.

A Passion Sequence

49   *Approaching the cross*
      Father,
      I approach the cross of your Son.
      Grant me your Holy Spirit
      that I may have a loving attention
      a serious and devout attention.

50   *The washing of feet*
      Dear Lord,
      Let me not forget you
      kneeling at the feet
      of your servants
      to wash their feet.

51   *The cup*
      Jesus,
      you drank and drained
      your cup of sorrow
      that our cup of joy
      might be full.

52 *Going out to Gethsemane*
Jesus,
teach me to follow you
without question, doubt or hesitation.

53 *At Gethsemane*
Flesh, be still
Soul, watch and pray.

54 *The Lord turned and looked at Peter*
My God, my God
look at me
that I may be pierced
and truly repent.

55 *The Passion*
Jesus,
what did you receive from us?
Curses, blows, a crown of thorns
a cross, nails, a spear in the side.
Remember that, my soul,
what Jesus received from you
And what you receive from Jesus.

56 *The Scourging*
Saviour,
forgive my sins
which were your stripes.

57 Jesus,
   by your stripes
   we are healed.
   Heal us and help us
   we humbly beseech you,
   Lord.

58 *The Crowning*
   Be silent, earth
   all flesh
   my heart.

   Jesus,
   crowned with thorns
   have mercy on us.

   You are the King of Glory
   O Christ – here –
   on the pavement.

   Let us not hide our faces
   from you
   for you did not hide your face
   from shame and spitting.

59 *The Carrying of the Cross*
   Jesus,
   you went out

carrying your cross for me.
Help me to go out
carrying my cross for you.

60 Jesus,
    by your holy cross
    help me to carry
    my cross.

61 Holy Face of Jesus! *(St Veronica)*

62 *The Nailing*
    What pain you suffered for me
    my Jesus!
    Help me to accept readily
    whatever pain
    I have to suffer.

63 *The Crucified*
    See my hands, feet, side, head, back?
    See my body given for you?
    See my blood shed for you?
    Yes,
    I see, Lord.
    What do you say
    to these things?

64   In view of the way
you were bashed and shattered
in your passion,
help me to be ready to take a bashing
– physically   – from accident
                    or illness
                    or violence
– mentally   – afflicted by others
                    or myself
– spiritually   – from dryness
                    or desolation
with something of your spirit
in some kind of real union
with you,
Lord Jesus Christ,
the Son of God.

65   Jesus Christ, crucified,
have mercy on us.

66   On the cross
from the cross
you embrace me with love.
You hold me up
and save me from falling.

67   *The fifth word*
      Jesus,
      by your thirst on the cross
      teach us how to fast
      and discipline ourselves.

68   *The seventh word*
      Father,
      you gave me my life.
      It is yours
      I give it back to you.

69*   *Prayers on the death of Jesus*
      by St Gertrude
      Let my soul find its refuge
      and shelter in you, O death,
      for you bring forth
      fruit of life eternal.

      Let me be buried and lost
      beneath the torrent of life
      that is ever gushing forth
      from you.

      Death, you are life eternal.
      Beneath your solemn shadow
      I dare to hope.

Absorb all my whole life
and let my own death
be merged and lost in you.

O mighty death
render mine calm and sure.
Death which brings life
let me dissolve away in you.

Triumphant death
from you shines forth
a love incomparable
in earth or heaven.

O death
so full of sweetness
be near to aid me
when my own death shall come.
In that dread moment
compass me round with your merits.

Be for me a sure way
that I fall not into the snare
as I step forth from this world.

Receive my soul then
and store it up
with the godly treasure
you have gathered.

May my life ebb away in you
so that in you
I may at length find rest.

You, then, were rich
yet for our sake you became poor
For us you suffered on the cross.

Wash us in the water
which flowed forth from your pierced side
and cleanse us from the stains
of our past life.

70   *The double flow*
Lord, Jesus Christ,
from your dead body
came forth life,
water and blood.
From the temple of your body
flowed the living stream
of water and blood.

71   Lord, Jesus Christ,
       as your body is our temple
       so it is our holy Sabbath
       our place of rest and peace
       Let us abide therein.

72   Like a tree
       planted by the waterside
       yielding its fruit in due season
       tree of the cross
       tree of life.

73   Through you,
       through your Cross and Passion
       through your Precious Blood,
       I enter into life,
       exercise faith.
       I enter into the prayer of life
       of faith.

The Resurrection

74   I rejoice in the Holy Spirit
       and in union with
       my Lord Jesus Christ.
       I cry through the same Spirit
       Abba, Father,
       you have glorified
       your Son.

I thank you, Father,
Lord of heaven and earth,
that you have glorified your Son
by raising him from the dead.

75 Jesus,
    Make me glad
    with the joy of your presence.

76 Jesus,
    in the power of the Holy Spirit
    I adore your sacred wounds.

77 Jesus,
    Lamb of God,
    Resurrection and Life.

78 Jesus,
    risen Lord,
    breathe into us
    your new life,
    the Holy Spirit.

79 Lord Jesus,
    I thank you
    for your paschal blessing
    of peace,
    the calmness of the Resurrection.

80 Jesus,
because you live
we also live.

81 Father,
you have glorified him
and will glorify him again.

82 I believe, confess and affirm
with praise and thanksgiving
that you have entered upon
and are now in your glory.

83 Jesus,
I am so glad
Because having suffered these things
you have entered into your glory.

84 In that light we always walked
but unaware
now
you are the Resurrection
and the Light of Life
breaks upon us like the dawn.

85 I want to be quiet before you
and receive your blessing of peace
Christ our Lord.

The Sacred Heart

86* Thank you, Father,
for giving us the Sacred Heart of Jesus
to pour forth on us
streams of mercy and grace.

That as it never ceased to burn
with love for us
so it might be a rest for the godly
and an open refuge of salvation
for the penitent.

87* O most sacred symbol
and sacrament of love
divine and human
in its fullness.

88* O sacred victim
opening wide
your Sacred Heart.

89* Sacred Heart of Jesus
burning with love for us,
opened wide for us:
pour forth on us
streams of mercy and grace.

90* Receive me,
     O my Jesus,
     into the abyss of your tender mercy
     and wash me from all stain
     in the great deep of your compassion.

91* O love,
     your self-oblation
     worthy of a God
     has opened to me
     the door of the most tender heart
     of my Jesus.

92* Most Sacred Heart of Jesus,
     have mercy on us.

93* *Various prayers to the Sacred Heart*
     Heart of Jesus,
     in you I trust.

     Heart of Jesus in the Blessed
     Sacrament,
     burning with love for us,
     inflame our hearts
     with love for you.

     Praised be the most Sacred Heart of Jesus
     in the Blessed Sacrament.

Heart of Jesus
in the Blessed Sacrament,
have mercy on us.

May the Sacred Heart of Jesus
be everywhere loved.

Sacred Heart of Jesus,
may your kingdom come.

94* May the Holy Spirit,
we beg you, Lord,
inflame us with that fire
which our Lord Jesus Christ
from the inmost sanctuary
of his heart
cast upon earth
and vehemently desired
to be enkindled.

95 Sacred Heart of Jesus,
burning with love for me,
kindle my heart with love for you,
that fire you came to cast
upon the earth
by giving us the Holy Spirit.

96* Jesus,
   meek and lowly of heart,
   make my heart
   like yours.

97* Fashion my heart
   like your Sacred Heart
   and then my whole life
   shall flow on in conformity
   with your good pleasure.

98* Let your bitter passion
   be my soft shade
   at the hour of my death
   and your heart
   which love has broken
   be my everlasting habitation.

99* Hail, wounded Heart of our
   Redeemer,
   thou art the image of
   the Heart of God the Father.

   Praised be the Holy Trinity
   and Honour to the one Heart
   whose wisdom brought all things
   into being
   in its love from all eternity.

Way, Life and Light

100*My soul give thanks to the Lord,
   all my being bless His holy name.
   My soul give thanks to Jesus,
   all my being bless his holy name.

101 Father,
   I want to express the holy name
   with all love, faith and devotion.
   JESUS.

102 In the Spirit
   I confess and express
   with faith, hope and love
   your holy name,
   JESUS.

103*You, Lord, are called Jesus
   that is to say a saviour.
   Be therefore my saviour
   and save me.

104 Jesus Christ our Lord,
   bring my whole self
   into subjection
   to the reign of your love.
   Establish your kingdom
   in my heart.

105 Jesus,
    through you
    we receive everything.
    We receive Holy Spirit.

106 Jesus,
    through you
    we go in and out
    and find pasture –
    Spirit, grace, life.

107 Jesus,
    you are the door and the way
    yours is the heart
    and yours the name
    to lead us to the
    calm and living and loving
    Godhead.

108 Jesus,
    Lead me
    (you are the shepherd).
    Let me enter through you
    (you are the door).
    Let me follow
    and walk in you
    (you are the way).

109* *Our Lord, to Julian of Norwich*
    I am the foundation
    of your praying.

110 Lord Jesus Christ,
    you are where I am.
    I am not yet where you are.

111 Jesus,
    if I have you
    I have everything
    whatever else I lack.
    If I do not have you
    I have nothing
    whatever else I have.

112 Jesus,
    if I abide in you
    I can do all things.
    Apart from you
    I can do nothing.

113 Jesus in me,
    perfect lover and adorer of God,
    love and adore God
    in me and through me.

114 Jesus in me,
   love God and my neighbour
   in me and through me.

115 O that Christ were more perfectly
   formed in me!
   O that the life of Christ in me
   were more fully expressed!

116 Jesus,
   your voice is like the sound
   of many waters
   because you cry
   through millions of hearts and
   mouths:
   FATHER.

117 Sacred Heart of Jesus
   Incarnation of love
   Epiphany of love

   Crucifixion of love
   Death and burial of love

   Resurrection of love
   Triumph of love

   Communication of love
   Communion of love
   Union of love.

118*Jesus,
    giver of salvation
    bestower of light
    and saviour of all.
    Guardian of the saints.
    Guide to eternal life.

119 I hunger and thirst for you,
    Jesus,
    my Lord and my God.

120 Jesus Christ,
    the Son of God,
    I adore you profoundly.
    I adore your Sacred Heart,
    your holy name.

121 Make yourself known to me
    in the breaking of
    the bread of life
    day by day,
    hour by hour.

The Jesus Prayer
122 Lord Jesus Christ,
    have mercy on me.

Lord Jesus Christ,
the Son of God,
have mercy on me,
a sinner.

123* Praying in the Spirit
within the love of God
we wait for your mercy,
Lord Jesus Christ.

124 Lord Jesus,
you have said,
'Yes I am coming soon.'
My heart says,
'Yes, come Lord Jesus.'

125 Heal me, Lord
and I shall be healed
Save me
and I shall be saved
for you are my praise.

126 God,
thank you for sending your
truth and your love –
Jesus.

127* May your peace be with me,
Jesus, true peace,
May I have evermore abounding
peace in you
So that through you
I may attain to that peace
which passes all understanding
Amidst which I shall behold you
in everlasting gladness
Amen.

128* Let us sing together simple praises
true hymns to Christ the King
as a precious fee
for his teaching of Life.

129 Let me rise up
in the judgement you have
commanded
rise up in the life and joy
you have given
rise up
in Jesus Christ,
the Resurrection and the Life.

130 In your temple
the temple of your Body
they all cry, Glory
in my room in your house
in my place, my space in your house
I cry with all of them, Glory.

131 Jesus, my master,
I come to you
to take your yoke upon me
and learn of you
and I shall find rest for my soul.

132*Jesus,
brightness of eternal glory
comfort of the pilgrim soul
with you my tongue is still
and my very silence speaks to you.

133 My dearest Lord and God,
as you broke open 'God'
break open me
open me out to you.

134 My heart is a womb
     a place prepared like Mary
     for you to be conceived,
     take root and grow.

135 Lead us to the heart of Godhead
     the heart of humanity
     the heart of life
     'where God is'
     (not away from life out of life but)
     deeper into life.

136 *To the Sacred Heart in the Blessed
     Sacrament*
     We worship you
     you worship God
     we worship God through you.

137* *Maranatha*
     Our Lord come
     to me
     from me
     through me.

138*The proper witness of my faith
   is he who said
   Father, all I have is yours
   and all you have is mine.
   My Lord Jesus Christ
   who is always in you,
   always coming from you,
   always with you
   and always God.

139*Life is in you
   and the life in you
   is light in us.

140*Life is in you
   and you are greater than it.
   Life is in us
   and it is greater than we
   and the life in you
   is the light in us.

141*All things are mine
   and I am yours
   and you are God's.

SPIRIT

142 Before, behind, beneath,
creation, conception, birth,
redemption
this prayer, this moment:
Creator Spirit.

143 Holy Spirit,
infinitude
eternally pouring forth,
energy of love
sustaining the universe.

144 *To the Holy Spirit, especially
at the beginning of prayer*
Blessed Spirit,
you conceive, create, quicken,
originate.
Do so to me, in me,
to my prayer, my life.

145 Come
Creator Spirit
Conceiving Spirit
Initiating Spirit
Life-giving
Birth-giving.

146 Spirit of co-(operation etc.)
        con-(versation etc.)
        comm-(unication etc.)

147 Spirit,
    Life-breath of love
    Fire of love.

148 Father,
    grant that I may pray in the Spirit
    walk in the Spirit
    be led by the Spirit
    be filled with the Spirit.

149 Holy Spirit,
    I pray for a sober estimate
    of this situation,
    of others
    and of myself.

150 I ask for
    the anointing and chrism
    of the Holy Spirit
    the holy oil of love, joy and peace.

151 I rejoice in you
    Holy Spirit
    and I entrust everything to you.

152 Descend
   holy dove.

153 Come, Holy Spirit,
   Bestow on me your gifts,
   Bring forth in me your fruits.

154 Uncreated Light
   move over the world
   your Church,
   my soul.

155 Holy Spirit,
   help my weakness.

156*Holy Spirit,
   give me life in your ways.

157 Breathe into me
   Breath of God.

158 O that I were filled
   with the Holy Spirit
   led and controlled
   by the Spirit.
   O that I were like Barnabas
   full of the Holy Spirit and faith.

159 Spirit
   lead me
   to Christ.

160 Jesus
   out of your Heart
   flow rivers of living water,
   the Holy Spirit.

161 It is you,
   Blest Spirit,
   who give me faith
   and the prayer of faith.

162 Come, Holy Ghost,
   I descend from the mind
   to the heart
   to Christ the centre of life.

163 Holy Spirit,
   help me
   pray for me
   with me
   through me.

164 Spirit,
   search and penetrate
   purify and heal
   at the deepest level.

MARY

165*Blessed are you,
  Mary, daughter of David,
  and blessed is the Fruit
  you have given us.
  Blessed the Father
  who sent his Son for our salvation
  and blessed the Holy Spirit
  who has taught us her mystery.
  Blessed be his name.

166 Mary,
  the Father was with you
  the Spirit came upon you
  and the Son was conceived in you.

167 Hail, Mary.
  God our Father was with you
  you conversed with his holy angel
  you were overshadowed by his Spirit
  you conceived and bore
  Jesus Christ the Son of God.

168*Higher than the cherubim
  more glorious than the seraphim,
  Mary, lead our praises
  Alleluia!

Bearer of the eternal Word
Most gracious magnify the Lord
Alleluia!

169 Mary,
you gave your Son
to the world,
to the cross,
to us.

170 Mary,
mother of sorrows
as well as joy and glory,
pray for us.

171*Woman,
not my mother only
but woman
in the widest sense
because of your great fruitfulness.

172*Holy Mary,
Queen of Heaven
and Lady of the world.

173*Queen of the world most worthy,
Mary, blessed Virgin,
pray for our peace and salvation;

you who brought forth
Christ the Lord,
the Saviour of all.

174* Mary,
   Mother of Grace
   Mother of Mercy
   hope of the oppressed
   light of the deep
   shrine of God.

175 Hail, Mary,
   full of grace
   full of the Holy Spirit
   and of faith:
   have mercy on us,
   pray for us
   your children.

176* Our Lady Mary
   sister and mother
   pray for me
   child and brother.

177* Mary,
   Mother of Grace
   Mother of Mercy
   strengthen us in all virtue

preserve us from all evil
protect us from all the enemies
of our souls.

178 *A Little Litany of Saint Mary the Virgin*
Our Lady of Bethlehem, pray for us,
Our Lady of Nazareth, pray for us,
Our Lady of Cana, pray for us,
Our Lady of Calvary, pray for us,
Our Lady of Pentecost, pray for us,
Our Lady of Glory, pray for us.

179 Holy Spirit,
help me to be ready
like Mary,
to receive whatever
God sends, says, gives or does;
to receive his Son.

180* Mary,
Mother of Grace,
Mother of Mercy,
protect us from the enemy,
receive us in the hour of death.

181 Blessed are you, Mary
Blessed your womb
your heart

your capacity for grace
for God
for love, truth and life.

182 May I receive your Word
As Mary received your Word.

183 Benign and gracious Lady
Mother, Sister,
pray for us.

Mother of joy, sorrow and glory
pray for us.

184 Create in me a clean heart, O God
and put a new and right spirit
within me
like the Virgin Mary
whose prayers I ask.

185 Mary,
may my end be like yours
that is,
in peace
in God, the Blessed Trinity
in the Communion of Saints.

186*Hail Mary,
    Mother of peaceful light
    pray for us, for me.

187*Fear not, Mary, alleluia
    for you have found favour with God
    alleluia
    you have found uncreated grace
    alleluia
    God himself became your Son
    alleluia
    with that grace you have found
    every uncreated good
    alleluia
    rejoice and be glad, Virgin Mary,
    alleluia
    for the Lord is with you and with us
    alleluia.

188*To thee we flee
    for shelter and compassion
    mother of God ...
    deliver us from danger.

189*Hail Mary, full of grace
    the Lord is with you
    the Holy Spirit too.

190* Hail beloved of the Lord
    seated by the highest
    hail God-receiving
    hail our link with the Saviour.

191 With Gabriel and the holy angels
    I salute you
    Mary
    the Mother of God.

RELATIONSHIP

192 Immense overwhelming
   overflowing
   lifting me up
   carrying me along –
   the prayer of the Communion of Saints.

193 You are
   therefore
   I am.

194 Fount of everlasting light
   draw me away to yourself
   into the ocean of your divine
   essence
   whence came forth the Word
   which spoke me into being.

195 Jesus,
   you and the Father
   you and us
   you and me.

196 First – you
   then – me
   then – consciousness of me
   then – consciousness of you.

197 First –
   you...your...yours
   love...grace...giving.
   Then – me
   existing ... receiving
   reacting ... responding.

198 It is not
   my life, my days.
   It is life.
   It is yours.
   It is all grace.

199 I receive everything:
   life,
   this day,
   sense impressions.

200 Lord God,
   I belong to you
   in every way
   by creation
   redemption
   sanctification.

   And you want me to belong to you
   out of choice
   because of love.

And you belong to me
because you give yourself to me
in love.

201 My God,
   you are in me.

202 Father,
   as you have made me
   your son
   and sent the Spirit of your Son
   into my heart
   grant that I may be led by the Spirit.

203 Father,
   you have set me free
   that I may be led by the Spirit
   in the freedom of Christ,
   that I may freely love and serve you,
   aspire to you
   and seek to be united to you.

204 O God,
   your love for us
   and ours for you
   are one:
   for our love for you
   is your gift.

205 Love of God in me:
    Love God through me.

206 All creatures
    show
    serve
    tend towards
    and lead us towards
    you,
    God.

207*Let all your wonderful works
    and all the gifts of your
    bounty to me
    bless you, glorify you and
    praise you
    for me,
    God of my life.

    Let your great and manifold mercies
    and all your infinite
    benefits to my soul
    bless you
    God of my heart.

    Let my inmost soul,
    my whole being and life
    bless you
    for you are the God of my salvation
    and my refuge.

208*How fair thou art, O Love,
   very essence of God.

209*Living God,
   your glowing love
   has a most attractive force
   which draws to your bosom
   all that your almighty hand
   has made.

210*How awesome is this place!
   This is none other than the
   house of God
   and this is the gate of heaven.

211 I want to thank God
   from the depths of my being
   and more –
   from the depths of God
   which underlie my being.

212 Father,
   thank you for giving me
   your Son.
   May he be most precious to us
   and loved by us.

213*Eternal Father
   look at me, I pray,
   because your only Son
   is crying to you
   from the midst of my heart.

214 Here you are
   in all your glory and majesty
   holiness and love.

215 Holy Spirit,
   you are praying for me and with
   me.
   Pray in me and through me.

216 What is life
   but waiting to die
   waiting for death
   waiting for you.

217 Come, Holy Spirit
   I descend from the mind to the heart
   to Christ
   the centre of life.

218*You rouse, awaken
   provide food and drink
   and send on a journey.

219 Virgin soul
virgin heart
meant for God
seeking God
being found by God
being formed by God.

220 There is
you
you and us
you in us.

221 I have embraced you
tasted you
wholly other
wholly here.

222 I rest in you
in deep untroubled peace.

223 You are the
aboriginal relatedness
source and origin
of relatedness
this is the tent of meeting.

224 Consciously receiving this present
from you
consciously receiving you
in this present.

225 I am free
just to be
in relation to you through
my fellow-creatures
your creatures
all that is
all created by you

free to worship you
without fear.

Eucharist
226 Receiving you
I receive all that is good
Mary and the saints;

God,
in giving me Jesus
you give me everything
that is good.

227*Come, saints,
    take the body of Christ,
    drinking what is holy
    the blood by which
    you are redeemed.

    Saved by the body and blood of
    Christ,
    refreshed by this,
    let us express our praises to God.

    Giver of salvation,
    Christ, the Son of God
    saved the world
    by his cross and blood.

    Bestower of light,
    Saviour of all
    you have lavished your glorious grace
    on believers.
    Let all who believe with a pure
    mind
    draw near
    let them take the eternal safeguard
    of their salvation.

Guardian of the saints
Guide to eternal life
you give freely
to those who believe.

You give the bread of heaven
to the hungry
You supply from the living fountain
the thirsty.

228*Come, Lord Jesus
    Come, bestower of light
    saviour of all
    Come, healer of souls
    fountain of all graces
    Come, guardian of the saints
    guide to eternal life
    Come, glory of the world
    joy of the heavens
    Come, Lord Jesus.

229*I was hungry
    and you gave me food:
    I was thirsty
    and you gave me drink:
    I was a stranger

and you welcomed me
I was naked
and you clothed me
I was sick
and you visited me
I was in prison
and you came to me.

230*Open your mouth wide
and I shall fill it.
So I did
(and my hands)
and received.

231 Father,
glorify your Son
even in me
for I have received him
today.

232 Thank you
for this daily bread for eternal life,
eternal bread
given here and now,
bread of the kingdom.

233*O God, you are my God,
    for you I long:
    for you my soul is thirsting.
    My body pines for you,
    like a dry, weary land without water.
    So I gaze on you in the sanctuary
    to see your strength and your glory.

    For your love is better than life.
    My lips will speak your praise
    so I will bless you all my life
    in your name I will lift up my hands.

    My soul shall be filled as with a banquet
    my mouth shall praise you with joy
    my soul is feasted as with marrow and fat.
    My mouth praises you with joyful lips
    for you have been my help.
    In the shadow of your wings I rejoice.

234*O God,
    the bread of our life,
    look upon us.
    Be the guardian of our bodies,
    be the saviour of our souls.

235* Defend, Lord, with your protection,
those whom you satisfy with
heavenly gifts,
that being set free from all things
hurtful
we may press onward with our
whole heart
to the salvation which comes from you.

236* Beyond belief
the wonder here contrived
but we believing Him
believe in it.

237* The blood that streams from Him
he pours into the chalice
the priest of the new dispensation
makes it a sacred oblation
the faithful take it and wash
themselves clean

one with the Father
now as of old
he opens his heart to the world.

238 When will you be inwardly transformed
by Christ, my soul?
Why should I not be when
I receive Christ so often
in Holy Communion?

When will you proclaim
this Gospel to others
by your changed life?

239 *Various acts of spiritual communion*
Father,
give us your Son.
Spirit,
open us to receive the Son.
Come,
Lord Jesus Christ,
the Son of God.

Father,
in the Holy Spirit
I ask for Jesus.

Like emerging from the tomb
emerge from within me
Jesus.

Emerge, light and life,
grace, power and love,
that I may continually receive you,
Jesus.

Jesus (with the lips)
Jesus (in the mind)
Jesus (in the heart).

RESPONDING

240*Awake, my soul
    awake and arise from the dust
    and come before the Lord your God.

241*This is the day which the Lord has made:
    we will be glad and rejoice in it.

242*Rejoice in his holy name!
    Let the heart of them rejoice
    that seek the Lord.

243 I aspire to you
    love, truth, light.

244*Lord,
    I stretch out my hands to you.
    My soul thirsts for you
    like a parched land.

245*With my whole heart
    I seek you.

246 O that I loved God
like Blessed Mary,
St John
and the other saints.

O that I loved him
like many thousands upon earth
at this very time.

247* See the Lord's servant.
Let it happen to me
as you have said.

248* In the morning
I offer you my prayer,
watching and waiting.

249* I will hear what the Lord God
has to say.
A voice that speaks of peace,
peace for his people and his friends
and those who turn to him
in their hearts.

250 Father,
in the name of Jesus,
in the Holy Spirit,
I offer my whole self
to you alone.

251 There is one thing I seek
   and that is God, Jesus.

   I am found
   I find Jesus, God.
   I am found by him.

   I do not seek
   points or considerations
   but God himself.

252 Father,
   I want to be
   wholly, directly, solely
   attentive and given to you.

253 Lord,
   I offer this meditation to you.
   Whatever you give,
   sweetness or dryness,
   I accept it all with thanks.

   This meditation
   is your work, gift and grace.
   My part is to give you myself.

254 Father,
   I ask for exactly that prayer
   which it is your will to give.

255 I will exercise myself
in the works of your hands
Prayer is a work of your hands
How manifold are your works of
prayer!

256 Speak, Lord
for your servant is listening
or if you are silent
let me still wait on you.

257 *When prayer is dry and difficult*
It does not matter
if I do not get 'consolation'

One thing matters –
your will,
union with Christ,
aspiration.

258 May I be troubled
by what ought to trouble me
and calm
before what ought to be accepted.

259 *In times of evil or adversity*
I thank you, Father
because out of this too
good will come.

260 Lord,
    let me seek
    not my success
    but your glory,
    what is true, right and good.

261*Put your trust in Him always:
    pour out your hearts before Him
    for God is our hope.

262*I will hope in Him
    I will hold firm and take heart.
    I will hope in the Lord.

263*Put your trust in the Lord
    and do good:
    dwell in the land
    and truly you will be fed.

264 My God,
    let me trust you
    and others in you and for you
    and myself in you and for you.

265 Let me learn humility
    from His humility
    and by receiving Him
    show it forth.

266 My God and my all,
   I offer, commit and resign to you
   in faith, hope and love
   through Jesus

   in the Holy Spirit
   myself, this event, others,
   with every circumstance and detail.

267 The one thing necessary,
   Father,
   is to do what you want
   at this time
   in this situation.

268 Father,
   In the name of Jesus
   I wait upon your will
   I seek your will.

269 Lord,
   I give myself to you
   in love –
   the love you gave to me.

270 Father,
   I am ready to suffer
   if it is your will.

271 Jesus,
   I look to the glory
   your glory
   our glory.

272 First of all
   before everything else
   and above all things
   I seek and ask for
   your praise, honour and glory.

273 Not many prayers and acts
   but one prayer, one reality
   One
   You.

274 *Basic prayer*
   No tricks, no games
   no time-filling words
   but just you only
   now
   here.

275 Mindfulness
of you
of others
of myself.

276*O happy place! When shall I be
my God, with thee, to see thy face?

277 Simple
single
prayer of nothing
nothing but you
waiting on you.

278 In the midst of this trouble and
tiredness
I will give thanks and praise
to you, my God.

279 I simply commit everything
to your personal and loving
Providence.

280 *After a big disappointment*
Christ is in me
I cannot despair
I am bound to hope.

PILGRIMAGE

281 O God,
    may your power rest on me
    may I rest in your power.
    Let me rest indeed
    but in you
    and in your power.

282 In my weakness
    let me find your strength.

283 Father,
    I stand (kneel/sit) before you.
    Draw my mind into my heart
    and my heart into
    the heart of Jesus,
    that I may pray
    in the Spirit
    from the heart.

284 Father,
    draw me
    to Jesus.

285*Lord,
    make us know your ways.
    Lord,
    teach me your paths.
    Make me walk in your truth
    and teach me
    for you are God my saviour.

286*My only refuge and strength,
    come quickly and sanctify
    all my works in me
    and grant me the aid and
    cooperation
    of your life-giving love.

287*Hear me when I call,
    God of my righteousness.

288 Lord,
    I am empty, fill me.
    I am helpless, help me.
    I am hungry, feed me.

289*O quicken me
    according to your word.

290* My soul cleaves to the dust:
     revive me according to your word.

291* I am yours,
      save me.

292* Lord,
      help me.
      Lord,
      save me.

293 *A cry for help*
     I simply pray
     for your healing grace
     for us all.

294 *In unavoidable affliction of any kind*
     Jesus,
     what I am carrying
     is not a chain
     but a cross.

     Help me to carry it
     as a cross
     behind you,
     with you.

295*O God, make speed to save us,
O Lord, make haste to help us.

Holy guardian angel
pray for me and help me.
I believe you do.

296*Create in me a clean heart,
O God,
and put a new and right spirit
within me.

297 Create in me a clean heart,
O God,
a heart and spirit of compassion
and concern for others,
especially those who suffer.

298*Give me to drink
the pure fresh water
of holy hope
that my soul may live.

299*God of hope,
fill us with all joy and peace,
in believing
that we may abound in hope
through the power of the Holy Spirit.

300 Lord,
   grant us a true love
   for God,
   our neighbours
   and ourselves.

301 Lord,
   give me
   a calm, cheerful
   courageous and charitable spirit.

302 Give me, O Lord,
   vigour of mind,
   energy of will,
   fervour of spirit.

303 *In adversity*
   Help me, Lord,
   to take this
   and not be overcome
   by despondency and defeatism –
   works of 'the devil'.

304*O Love,
   you are constant, strong, invincible.
   Teach me constancy in loving Jesus
   and unfaltering perseverance
   in serving him.

305 *In contention with others*
   I resign myself to your will
   and ask for that inward peace and
   security
   which comes from your love,
   presence and grace,
   and that I may look upon all
   with a sincere love and good will.

306 Help me to tread the path
   on which you have set my feet:
   the way of conversion,
   away from cowardice
   and towards courage.

307 Perfect love:
   cast out my fear.

308 St Raphael,
   angel of healing and journeys
   bless and prosper our way
   before God.

309 Lord,
   increase my faith
   may I abound in hope
   and grow in love.

310*Heal us, O Lord,
and we shall be healed
save us
and we shall be saved
for you are our praise.

Regarding Death

311 Father,
I commit and resign
into your hands
and accept from your hands
the time, place and manner
of my death:

And my desire and intention is
that I should then
commit and resign
my soul, my life
into your hands.

312*I will fall asleep in the Heart of Jesus
the source of supreme and true peace
When at length I breathe my last
I will place my heart in His
opened Side
I will confide my heart to His Heart.

313* *Some prayers of St Gertrude*

(a)   Under your protection
I will calmly await the moment
when I shall return to God
and give back my spirit
to Him who gave it.

(b)   Let me lose my fleeting life
in yours
which is eternal,
God of my life.

(c)   O Love,
set on the hour of my death
the seal of your tenderness

(d)   Impress upon it
the stamp of your boundless,
unfailing mercy.

(e)   May your abounding blessing
go with me
and in its strength
may I triumph over
every foe and every hindrance

(f) till I come to you
to joy which fades not
to a possession which has no end.

(g) O Love,
much-loved evening-tide,
at the hour of my death
cheer and gladden me
with the sight of you.

(h) At that dread moment
let the sacred flame
which burns evermore
in your divine essence
consume all the stains
of my mortal life.

(i) My calm and peaceful evening,
when the evening-time of my life
shall come,
give me to sleep in you
in tranquil sleep.

(j)   O Love,
        when the shadows of evening
        fall upon my life,
        deign to shine forth on me
        as the morning dawn
        and when I lie down in death,
        give me to draw eternal life
        from you.

314*God is eternal light
        May I die at peace with my God;
        Lord, stay by our door.

END-PRAYER

315 Mysterious in yourself,
     manifest in your disclosing.

316*O Love,
     who art very God
     amidst the crash and ruin of earth
     open to my soul
     a sure refuge in thee.

317 What do I want?
     to fall into the abyss of your light
     to be lost in your light.

318 Falling into flame
     flame of falling light.

319 Pure act
     pure being
     pure love
     pure giving.

320*A stream flows murmuring inside me;
     deep down in me it says –
     come to the Father.

321 Let me go again about the garden
entering with Christ
a thief from another tree.

322 I it am *(Jesus, according to*
Julian of Norwich)
you are it.

323 Everything that is not you
is created by you
and that means everything.

324*You
Lord our God
you
the Lord
are one
you are
the one.

325 There is an other
there is one who
one who is greater than

you are the other
you are the one who
you are greater than.

326 You are the one who
you are the one
you are the
you are
you.

327 You are the other
the next
the answer to the question
ever recurring
'And then....?'

328 Prayer is addressed words
addressed thoughts
addressed silence
addressed to you
meant for you
offered to you,
my God,
worshipful God.

APPENDIX

SOURCES OF PRAYERS
MARKED * IN TEXT

No	Source
4	Col:1.13
9	Eph:3:14-19
13	John 12:28
14	John 17:1
18	*The Exercises of St Gertrude,* Burns & Oates, 1863
19	James 3:17
20	2 Cor:1:3
21	Luke 10:21
22	Eccles 23:4
33	Brihadaranyaka Upanishad III
44	Medieval hymn quoted by Pierre Charles, *Prayer For All Times,* 3rd series, XLIV.
46	Julian of Norwich, *A Revelation of Love.* ch. 26 (University of Exeter ed.)
69	Exercises
86	Roman Missal
87	Cardinal Newman, *Meditation on the Sacred Heart*
88	*The Exercises of St Gertrude,* Burns & Oates, 1863
89	Preface of the Mass to the Sacred Heart, Old Roman Missal
90	St Gertrude
91	St Gertrude
92	Roman Missal
93	Various 'indulgenced prayers'

262   Ps 27:14
263   Ps 37:3 *(Book of Common Prayer)*
276   English Hymnal, 411 (17th century)
285   Ps 25:4-5 (Grail Translation)
286   St Gertrude
287   Ps 4:1 *(Book of Common Prayer)*
289   Ps 119:25 *(Book of Common Prayer)*
290   As 289
291   Ps 119:94
292   Matt 15, 25; 14, 30
295   cf. Psalms 40:13 & 70:1 *(Book of Common Prayer Office)*
296   Ps 51:10
298   St Gertrude
299   Rm 15:13
304   St Gertrude
310   Jer 17:14
312   Lanspergius (16th century)
313   Exercises
314   4th century. Early Christian Prayers, 88
316   St Gertrude
320   St Ignatius of Antioch + c.107. Early Christian
      Prayers, 29
324   Deut 6:4 (= the Jewish *Shema*)